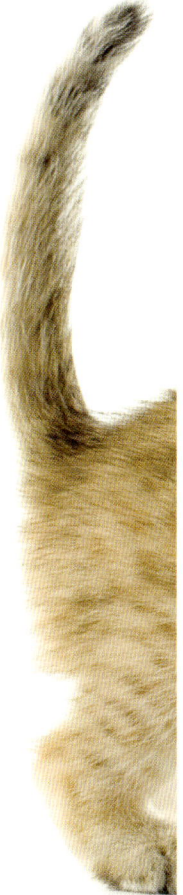

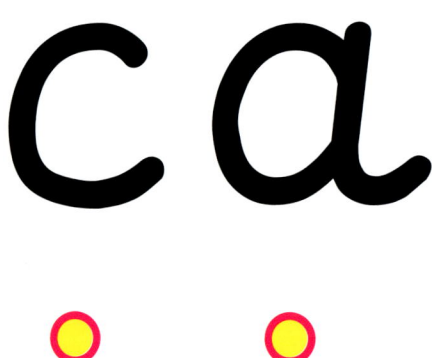

Step-by-Step Mini Words

Can you say the sounds of these letters?

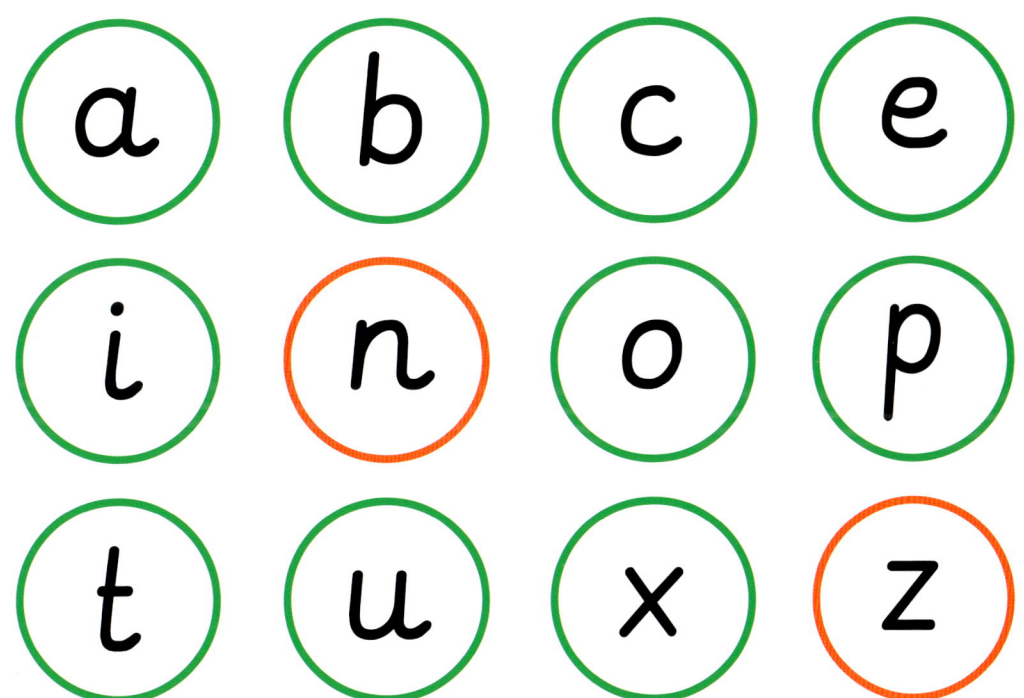

C

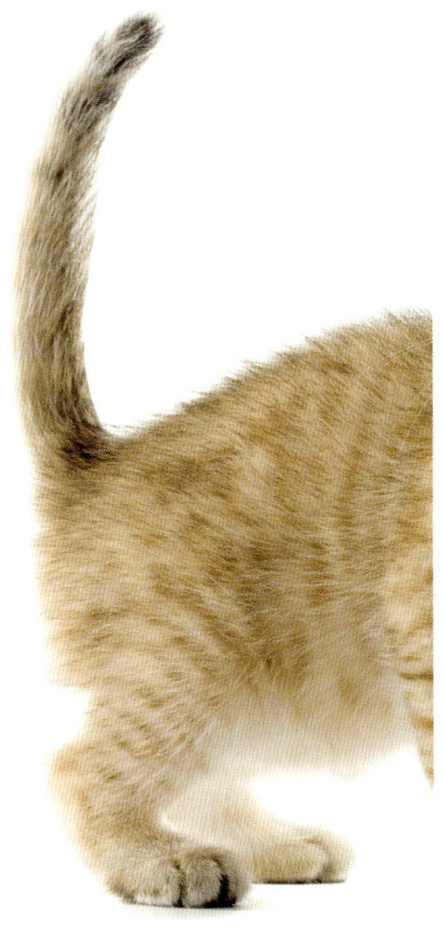

cat

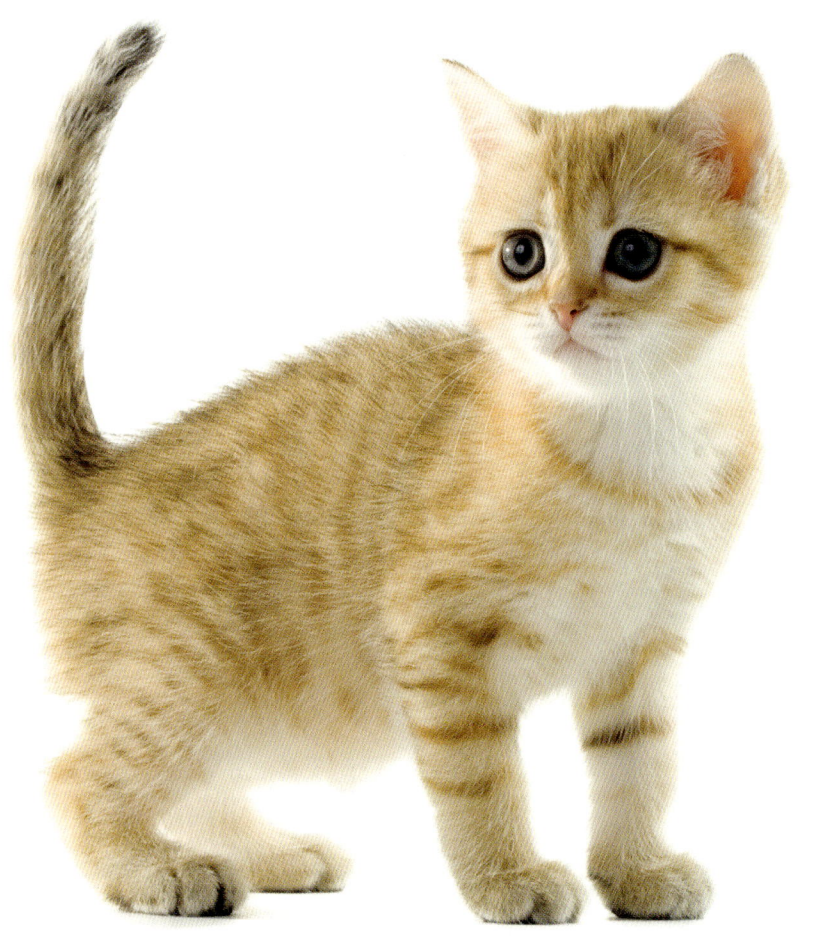

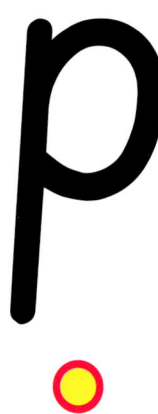

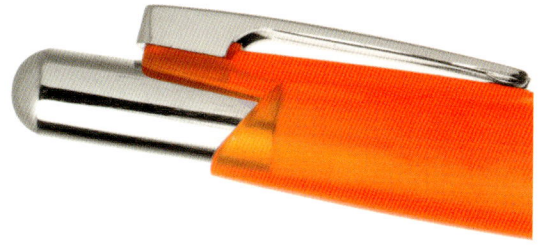

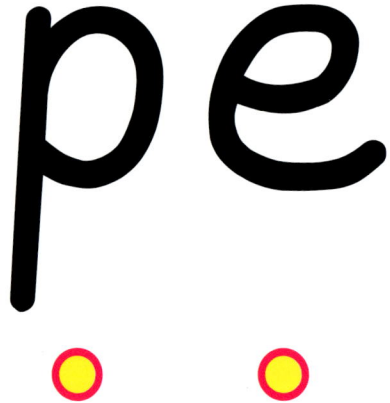

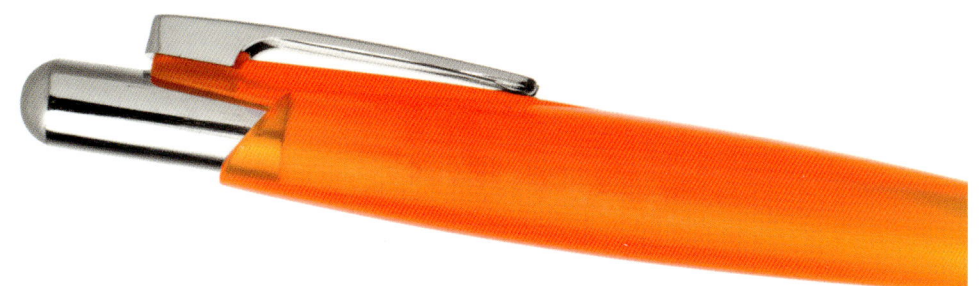

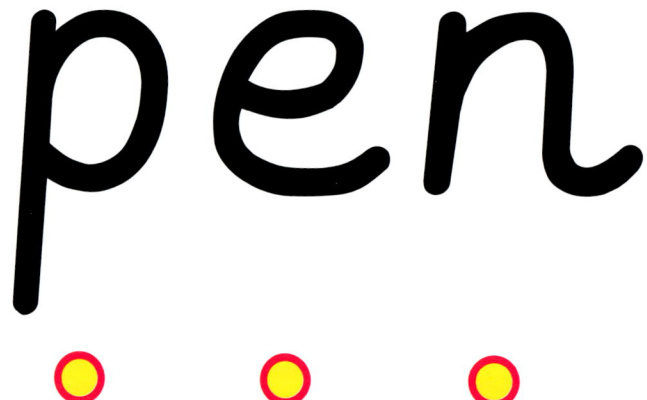

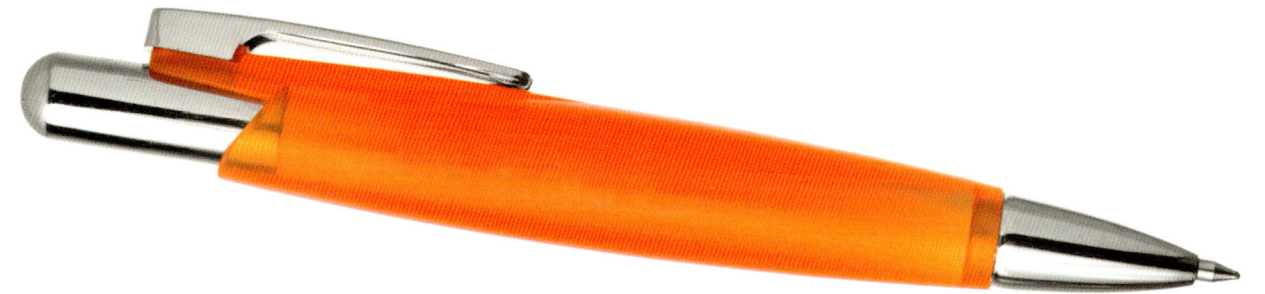

z

○

14

15

zi

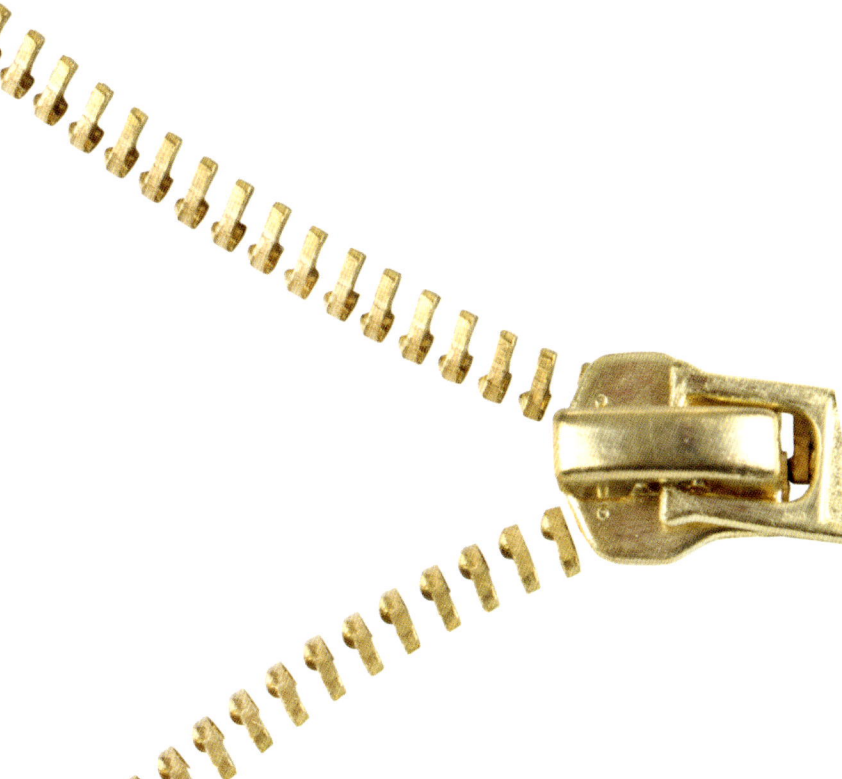

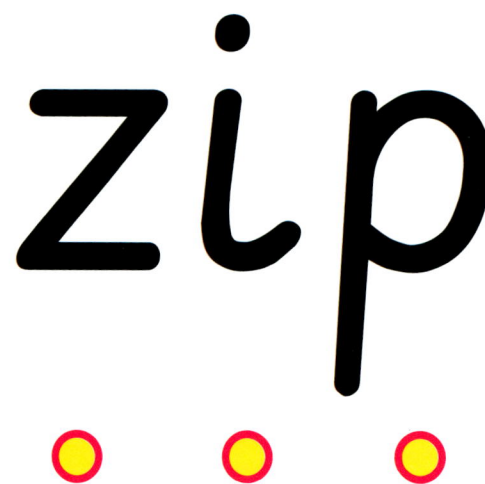

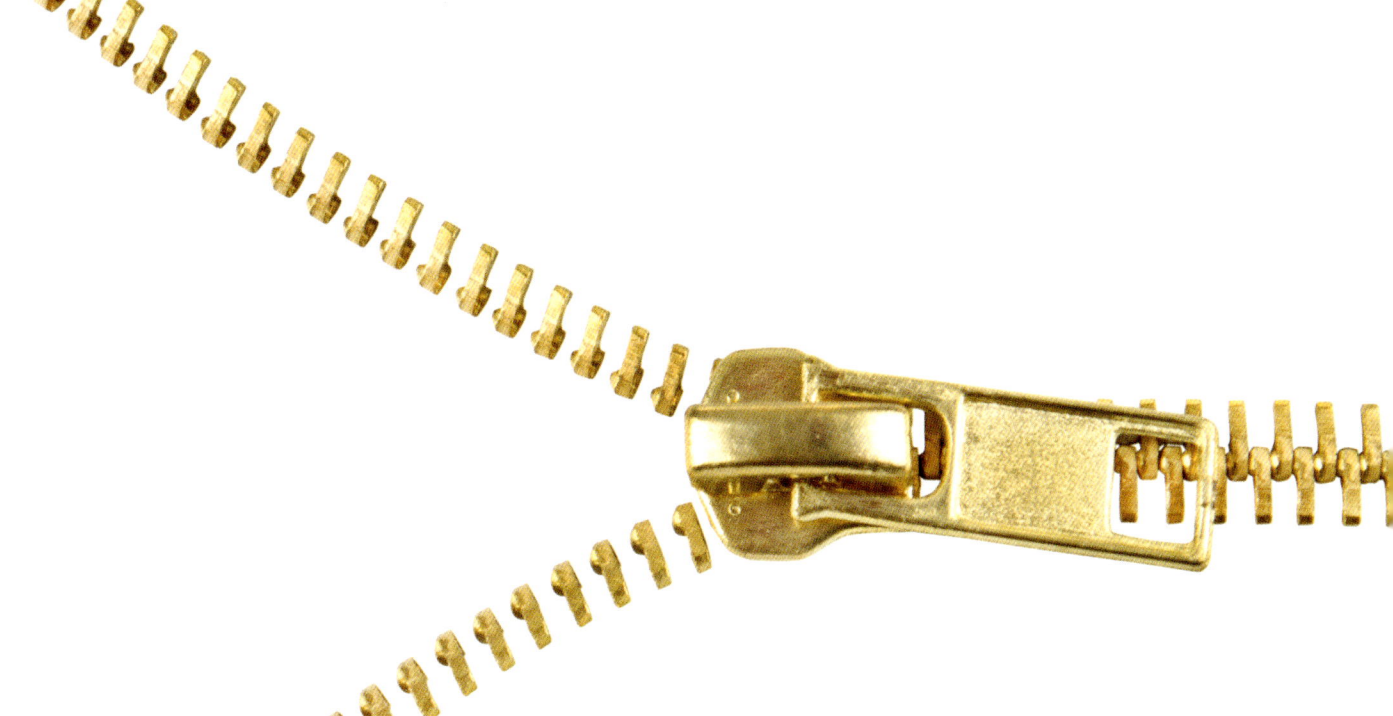

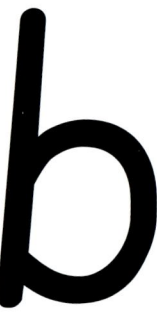

bo

box

○ ○ ○

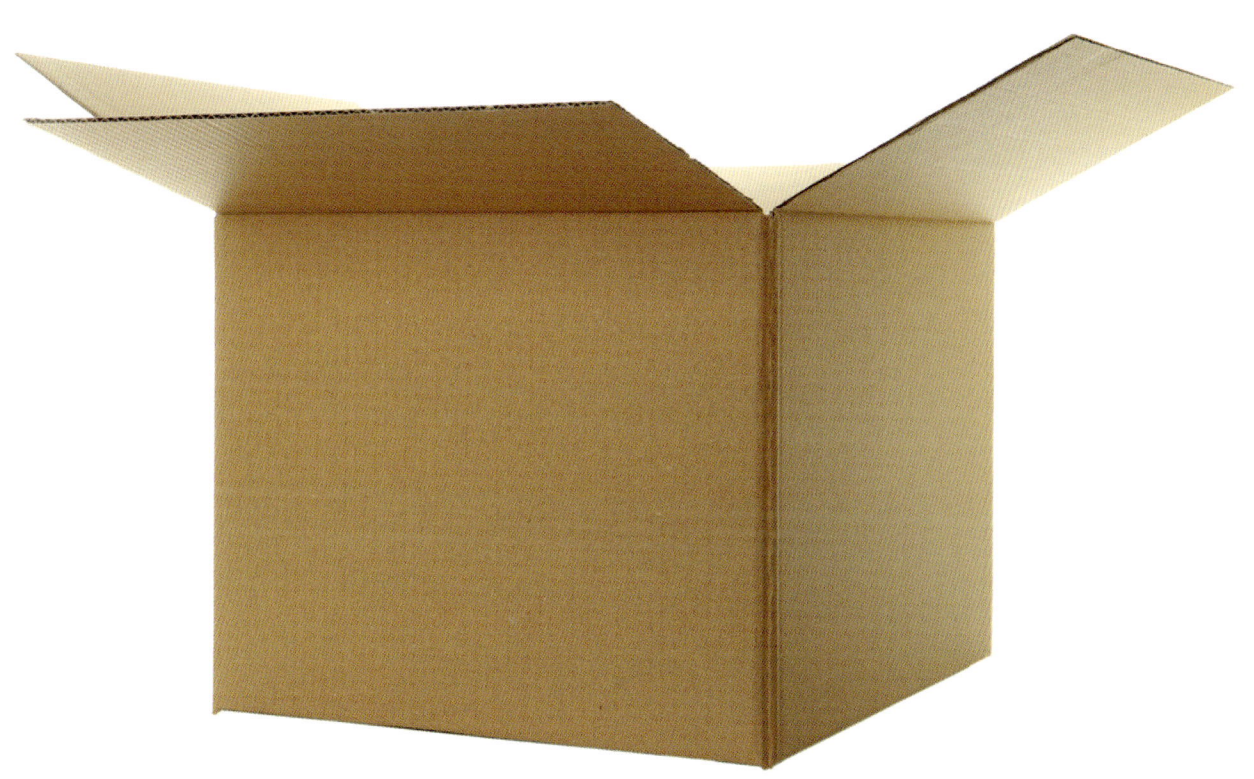

C

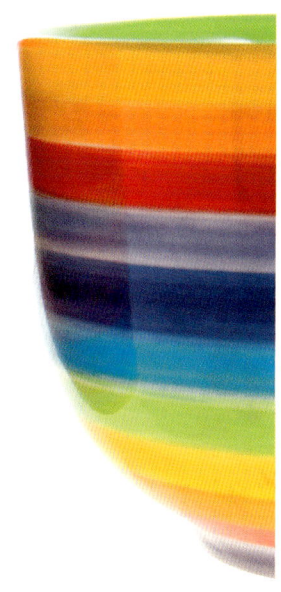

cu

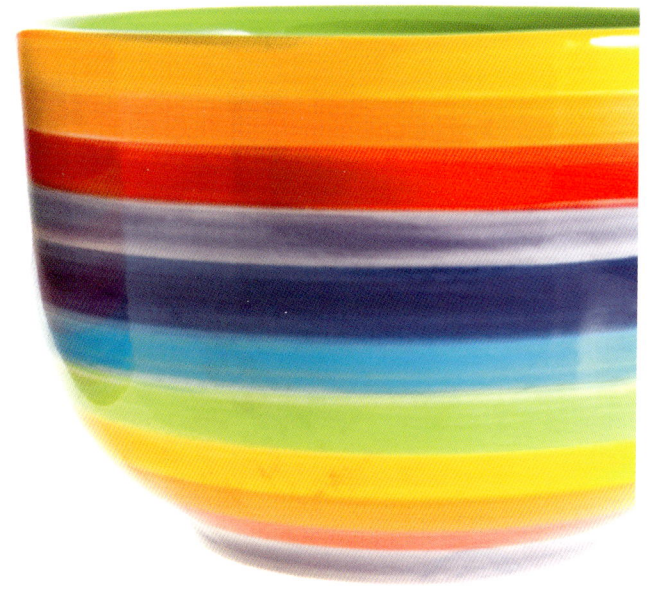

cup

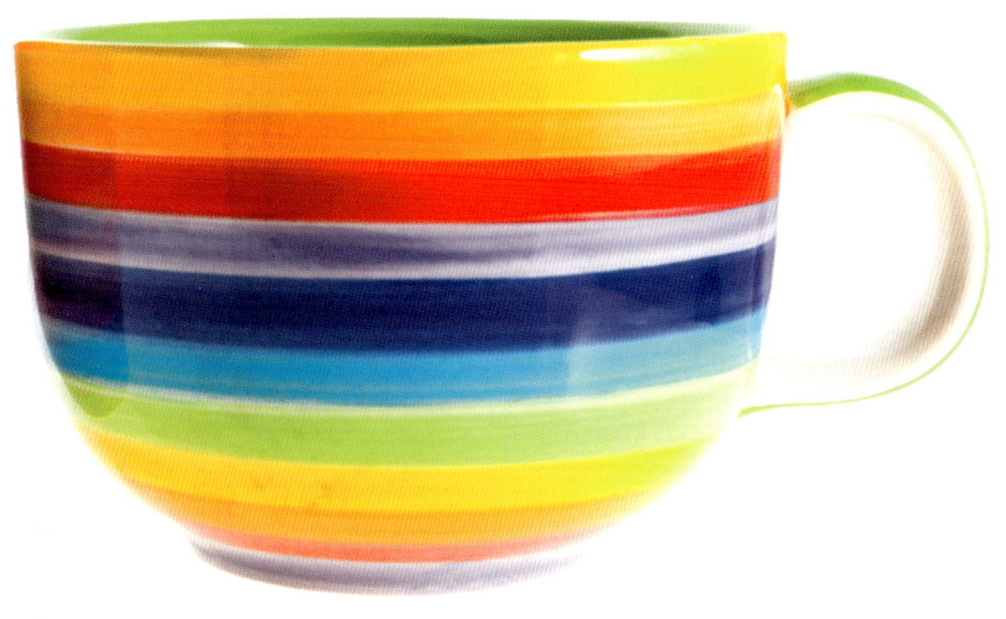

Can you read these words?

cat

bat

pen

hen

zip

lip

box

fox

cup

pup

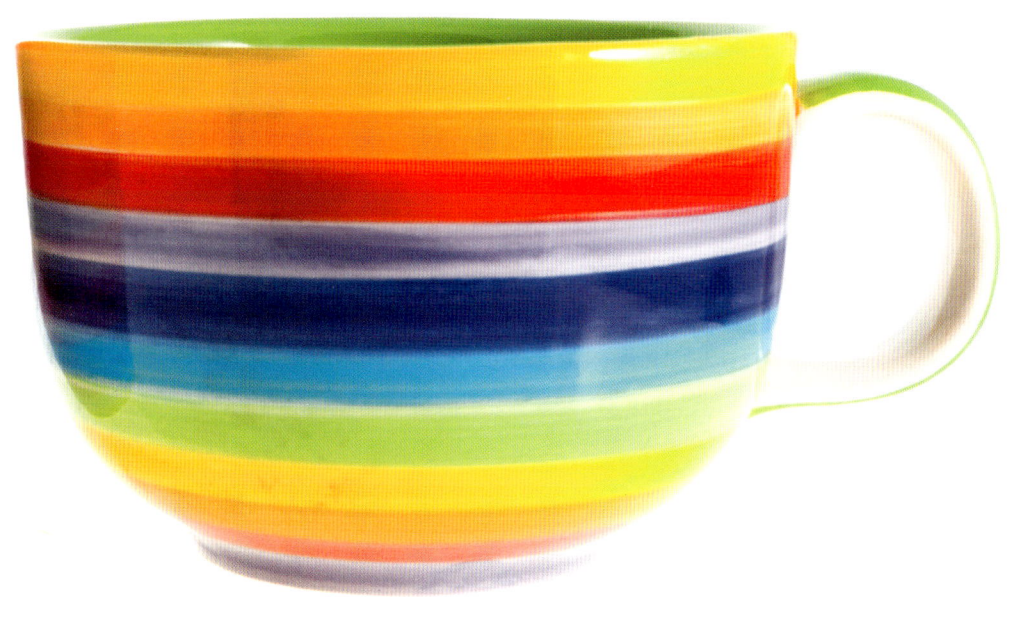

31

Can you read these words?

cat

pen

zip

box

cup

bat

hen

lip

fox

pup